Published by Adventurous Publishing
Copyright © 2024 Lionel Graves

Paperback ISBN: 978-1-915862-48-8

Welcome to this edition on

Handling conflict

Ft Lionel Graves

Contents

THE B!G QUESTION.

The Big Question is a brand that delve's deep into the minds of influential leaders and uncover their strategies through asking Big questions.

We believe that the journey from aspiration to achievement is both fascinating and instructive.

By asking leaders profound questions about their experiences, we gain valuable insights that can guide you in turning your own dreams into tangible outcomes.

Welcome to this edition in The Big Question book series on Handling conflict.

In this book, we speak to Lionel Graves, a boxer, actor and private security specialist.

We'll look at the Graves story, and why de-escalation is so important.

Introduction

Beginnings

Conflict is an inevitable part of human life. Whether it's a minor disagreement with a coworker, a misunderstanding with a friend, or a heated exchange with a stranger, we encounter countless conflicts throughout our lives.

Research suggests that the average person experiences numerous interpersonal conflicts each week, many of which are handled poorly. In the heat of the moment, emotions often override rational thinking, leading to escalated tensions and unresolved issues.

In this book, I share insights drawn from my journey through martial arts and security, emphasizing the critical importance of de-escalation. Drawing on years of experience in high-pressure environments, I will guide you through practical strategies for recognizing potential conflicts and diffusing them before they spiral out of control.

You will learn that de-escalation is not merely a technique; it is a mindset rooted in awareness, discipline, and empathy. By understanding the principles of de-escalation, you can transform your approach to conflict, leading to better outcomes in both your personal and professional interactions.

This book aims to equip you with the tools needed to navigate conflicts with calmness and confidence, allowing you to foster a more peaceful and harmonious life.

Join me on this journey as we explore the art of de-escalation and discover how choosing peace can change the way we engage with the world around us.

Chapter *one*

Origins

My journey into security wasn't meticulously planned or dreamt about as a child. I never woke up one morning thinking, "I want to be a security guard." Instead, my path began in a much different arena—martial arts. About 25 years ago, I first dipped my toes into the world of kickboxing.

While I wasn't the best, I could hold my own in the ring, and I had my fair share of fights. One of my fondest memories was facing off against Idris Elba for a series on the Discovery Channel, where I showcased my skills in front of a wider audience. Additionally, I fought in Thailand, cherishing experiences that I wouldn't trade for the world.

Over the years, I have built a successful career not just as a martial artist but also as a seasoned security professional. Based in Amsterdam, I have worked in various high-pressure environments, primarily focusing on protecting VIPs and celebrities. My extensive background in martial arts has been instrumental in shaping my philosophy around conflict resolution, particularly the importance of de-escalation techniques.

Before long, martial arts evolved from a personal passion into a career. I opened a small shop selling boxing gloves and martial arts gear, never intending to start a gym. Yet, demand found me. People would come to my store asking, "Why don't you teach us?" Initially, I resisted; training wasn't my goal. However, I eventually acquiesced.

I began teaching inside the store on a small mat where people could try out the equipment. Soon, 16 students were crammed into my shop for classes. The unexpected demand continued to grow, necessitating a larger space. Before I knew it, I had a full-fledged gym housed in a high-profile hotel—Van der Valk.

Despite its success, the gym consumed all my time. My freedom felt compromised; I found myself tethered to the gym day and night, unable to take holidays or even enjoy a day at the beach.

I made a decision—I wanted my life back.

Chapter *two*

Finding Purpose

When I sold the gym about six months ago, I decided to focus on a different path that was already familiar to me: security. I had been doing security work on the side for over 20 years, so this transition felt natural. Unlike the gym, this path offered more freedom.

Today, I work as a security guard, primarily for artists and celebrities, ensuring their safety on stage or at events. This role demands vigilance and readiness, but it also brings its own set of challenges and rewards.

One key realization in security is that nothing happens —at least not on my watch. I see potential issues before they unfold. When I'm with an artist, I can spot the individual in the crowd who's about to cause trouble or sense when someone is gearing up to jump on stage.

The key is to identify these threats before they escalate. That's what led me to understand the importance of de-escalation.

In security, particularly in high-profile environments, situations can spiral out of control quickly. Emotions run high, especially in crowds where people may be under the influence or simply overly excited. The ability to de-escalate is not just an advantage—it's a necessity.

Chapter *three*

—

De-escalation at it's finest

One night, a man entered a venue where I was working. He was only five meters away from me, and I sensed something wasn't right. Sure enough, he had just fired a gun.

Rather than panicking or escalating the situation, I approached him calmly. "Hey, my friend," I said, "you should leave. The police are on their way. Take that door." I showed him an exit route, and he walked out peacefully.

That night could have ended very differently. Had I taken a more aggressive approach—holding him down or waiting for the police to arrive—it could have jeopardized my life and the lives of others.

De-escalation wasn't about being passive; it was about being smart, about keeping everyone safe without unnecessary conflict.

According to a 2021 study by the International Association of Chiefs of Police (IACP), de-escalation techniques reduce the likelihood of violent confrontations by 60%.

When people are already on edge, reacting with aggression will only heighten their emotional state. My approach, which I like to call the "low flame technique," prevents situations from boiling over. The focus is on diffusing tension, not adding to it.

Chapter *four*

Principles

Martial arts played a pivotal role in shaping my view of confrontation. It's about discipline, not just physical strength. In a fight, being reactive can get you knocked out. But remaining calm and strategic can save you. The same principles apply to security.

In martial arts, the principle of staying calm under pressure translates well to de-escalation. You must be aware of your surroundings, reading people's body language and understanding what might trigger them. In martial arts, you train to be quick and sharp, both physically and mentally; this skill set has proven invaluable in my security work.

Research from the Journal of Police and Criminal Psychology indicates that professionals who practice mindfulness and self-discipline are 37% more effective at managing volatile situations.

Security, much like martial arts, is about being quick —mentally more than physically. It's about recognizing a problem before it arises and knowing how to neutralize it.

Many people think leadership is about commanding respect, but to me, it's about supporting others. I've always been a protector, even as a child growing up without a father. I looked out for my mother and siblings, and that protective instinct has carried through into my adult life. In both martial arts and security, my goal is to help, not hurt.

I've learned that sometimes the best leadership comes from below. When you're always looking out for others, not for yourself, you develop a natural authority that people respect. It's not about ego or power; it's about being there for people when they need you.

A study by Gallup found that employees who feel supported by their leaders are 59% more likely to stay at their jobs and 29% more productive.

This principle applies not only in the workplace but in any situation where human emotions run high. People don't need domination; they need support.

As we look to the future of security—and even beyond that, to daily life—the importance of de-escalation cannot be overstated. Conflict is pervasive. Whether in personal relationships, at work, or on a global scale, people are continually clashing. But what if we approached conflict with a mindset of de-escalation, rather than escalation?

The success of books like Verbal Judo by George Thompson and The Gift of Fear by Gavin de Becker underscores the growing recognition of de-escalation across various industries. These books emphasize that violence and conflict aren't inevitable outcomes. There's always a way to talk someone down and find a peaceful resolution.

In my experience, the results speak for themselves. I've defused countless situations—whether guiding a gunman out of a venue or stopping two individuals from fighting—without resorting to force.

That's what I want to impart: the understanding that de-escalation is not just a technique; it's a mindset.

My big question to you is...

Are you happy with the way you're handling conflict in your *life?*

About the author

Lionel Graves is a Dutch kickboxer and actor known for his contributions to the sport and the entertainment industry. He gained widespread attention after facing Idris Elba in the actor's professional kickboxing debut, held at London's York Hall.

Outside the ring, Lionel has appeared in films such as Lux Life, Mr. Frog (2016), and Sunny Side Up (2015). His career bridges both physical and creative disciplines, showcasing his versatility as a fighter and performer.

Be **you**,
be **bold**,
Go **big**.

TBQ

Notes

................Go big

_____

_____

_____

_____

_____

_____

_____

_____

_____

_____

_____

_____

_____

_____

_____...............Go big

..............Go big

_____

_____

_____

_____

_____

_____

_____

_____

_____

_____

_____

_____

_____

_____

_____

_____

_____

_____...............Go big

.............Go big

...............Go big

_____
_____
_____
_____
_____
_____
_____
_____
_____
_____
_____
_____
_____
_____
_____
_____
_____...............Go big

..............Go big

...............Go big

...............Go big

...............Go big

_____

_____

_____

_____

_____

_____

_____

_____

_____

_____

_____

_____

_____

_____

_____

..............Go big

...............Go big

...............Go big

_____
_____
_____
_____
_____
_____
_____
_____
_____
_____
_____
_____
_____
_____
..............Go big
_____

_____

_____

_____

_____

_____

_____

_____

_____

_____

_____

_____

_____

_____

_____

_____

..............Go big

...............Go big

_____
_____
_____
_____
_____
_____
_____
_____
_____
_____
_____
_____
_____
_____..............Go big

...............Go big

_____

_____

_____

_____

_____

_____

_____

_____

_____

_____

_____

_____

_____

_____

_____

_____

_____

_____..............Go big

_____

_____

_____

_____

_____

_____

_____

_____

_____

_____

_____

_____

_____

_____

_____

_____...............Go big

.............Go big

...............Go big

_____
_____
_____
_____
_____
_____
_____
_____
_____
_____
_____
_____
_____
_____
_____
..............Go big

_____

_____

_____

_____

_____

_____

_____

_____

_____

_____

_____

_____

_____

_____

_____

_____

..............Go big

_____

_____

_____

_____

_____

_____

_____

_____

_____

_____

_____

_____

_____

..............Go big

..............Go big

_____

_____

_____

_____

_____

_____

_____

_____

_____

_____

_____

_____

_____

_____

..............Go big

..............Go big

_____

_____

_____

_____

_____

_____

_____

_____

_____

_____

_____

_____

_____

_____

_____

_____

...............Go big

_____
_____
_____
_____
_____
_____
_____
_____
_____
_____
_____
_____
_____
_____
_____
_____
_____..............Go big

...............Go big

_____
_____
_____
_____
_____
_____
_____
_____
_____
_____
_____
_____
_____
_____
_____
_____...............Go big

............Go big

...............Go big

_____

_____

_____

_____

_____

_____

_____

_____

_____

_____

_____

_____

_____

_____

_____

_____

..............Go big

The Big Question

@thebigquestionhq

www.ingramcontent.com/pod-product-compliance
Lightning Source LLC
LaVergne TN
LVHW022013080426
835513LV00009B/693